D1257849

tHE MIRACLE CHILD

Told by Elizabeth Laird with Abba Aregawi Wolde Gabriel

A STORY FROM ETHIOPIA

Holt, Rinehart and Winston
New York

The author would like to thank all those who have advised on and
contributed to the making of this book, especially the staff of The British Library,
the Reverend R. W. Cowley, David McDowall, Oxfam, Alan Peacock,
and Dr. Richard Pankhurst.

The illustrations in this book are taken from
an eighteenth-century manuscript in a collection
of Ethiopian manuscripts in London.

Illustrations photographed by Angelo Hornak.

Text copyright © 1985 by Elizabeth Laird
Illustrations copyright © 1985 by William Collins Sons and Co., Ltd.
First published in the United States in 1985 by
Holt, Rinehart and Winston, 383 Madison Avenue,
New York, New York 10017.

Library of Congress Catalog Card Number: 85-45374
Library of Congress Cataloging in Publication Data is available.

ISBN: 0-03-006052-4

First American Edition

Printed in Belgium by Henri Proost and Cie
1 3 5 7 9 10 8 6 4 2

ISBN 0-03-006052-4

ስብሐት፡ለእግዚ፡ ስብሐት፡ለወልድ፡
ስብሐት፡ለመንፈስ፡ ቅዱስ፡ ፫ ጊዜ በል፡፡
ስብሐት፡ለእግዝእትነ፡ ማርያም፡ ድንግል፡
ወላዲተ፡ እየሱስ፡ ስብሐት፡ለመስቀሉ፡ እግዚ
እነ፡ ኢየሱስ፡ ክርስቶስ፡፡ ክርስቶስ፡ በያሕሬቱ፡
ይዘከረነ፡እመንዳግም፡ ይጹእቱ፡ ኢያስተሐዋለነ
ለስብሐተ፡ ስሙ፡ ያንቅሐነ፡፡ ወበእ ያዕሉነቲ፡ ያጹ
ነዐነ፡፡እግዝእትነ፡ ማርያም፡ አዕርጊ፡ ፀሎተነ፡፡
ወእስተ ሥራቱ፡ ጋሚአተነ፡ ቅድመ፡ መንበሩ፡
ለእግዚእነ፡፡ለዘእብልዐነ፡ ዘንተ፡ ኅብስተ፡ ወለዘ
እስተ፨ ዘነተ፡ ጽዋዐ፡ ወለዘወሰረ፡ለነ፡ ሲሳየነ
ወእራዘነ፡ ወለ ዘፈጸኘለ፡ ለነ፡ ንዋ፡ ጋሚአተነ፡
ወለዘወሀበነ፡ ሥጋ ሁ፡ ቅዱሰ፡ ወደ ሞ፡ ክቡረ
ወለዘእብጽሐነ፡ እስከ፡ ዛቲ፡ ሰዓተ፡ ነሁ፡ ክሞ፡
ስብሐተ፡ ወእነተ ቴቱ፡ለእዚእብሐቶር፡ ሲ ውሱ፡
ወለ ወላዲቱ፡ ድንግሉ፡፡ ወለመስቀሉ፡ ክቡር፡
ይትእነ ተ፡ ወደቤጋሉ፡ ስሙ፡ ለእግዚእብሐቶር፡
ወትሪ፡ በ ኵሉ ጊዜ፡ ወለ ኵሉ፡ ሰዓተ፡፡

Transcribed by Abba Aregawi Wolde Gabriel
Priest of the Ethiopian Orthodox Church

This prayer is written in Geez, the language of the
Ethiopian church. It is used at the Festival of St. Tekla
Haymanot, and on other special Saint's Days. In the
prayer, the priest gives glory and praise to God the Most
High, and to the Virgin Mother and to his venerable
Cross. He begs that our prayer may rise before the
throne of our Lord.

"Of him who has given us to eat this bread,
Of him who has given us to drink this cup,
Of him who has prepared for us our food
and our clothing."

If you go to Egypt and travel down the Nile, you will pass pyramids, temples, green fields and empty deserts. But if you go on and on, following the curve of the river, you will come at last to mountains that tower up above you. And if you climb up them, higher and higher, through dense forest and thick clouds, you will come to a beautiful high plateau, where even higher mountains rise up into the sky. And that is the land of Ethiopia.

Ethiopia has a special history, because it is one of the oldest Christian countries in the world. There were small groups of Christians there from the very earliest times. In the fourth century, two young Syrian boys landed on the Red Sea coast of Ethiopia. The inhabitants captured them, and took them to the king. They became his trusted servants, and when he died, they looked after his infant son. The new king grew up to be a Christian, and from that time to this, Christianity has been the state religion and churches have flourished throughout the land.

In the olden days, before there were trains and airplanes, it was very hard to get to Ethiopia. Only a few intrepid travelers climbed the steep paths to the hidden land in the mountains. So the people of Ethiopia were undisturbed by the rest of the world. They worshipped in their own special way, they told their own special stories and they painted their own very special pictures, some of which you can see in this book.

The people who wrote the books and painted the pictures were monks, living in monasteries high up on the mountain tops. They did not have paper, so they made their books from cow and sheepskin, and wrote them out by hand, in the same way that medieval monks in Europe did. Some of their stories are about the Bible characters we know: Adam and Eve,

Solomon and the Queen of Sheba, the baby Jesus at Bethlehem. But the Ethiopians also had their own stories, about saints and kings, battles and victories, miracles and mysteries.

The story in this book is about a very famous Ethiopian saint called Tekla Haymanot. He lived seven hundred years ago, in the thirteenth century, and he founded Ethiopia's greatest monastery at Debra Libanos, where many monks still live and work. When he lived, he was greatly loved, and after he died, monks wrote down the stories that were told about him, and painted beautiful pictures to illustrate his life. We do not know the name of the man who painted the pictures in this book, but we do know that he lived two hundred years ago, sometime in the eighteenth century.

The story of St. Tekla Haymanot is still told in Ethiopia. Children learn from the priests about the saint who stood on one leg, and the miraculous child who provided food when a terrible famine was in the land.

This picture shows Saga Zaab bringing an offering to the church. The priest is carrying a cross in one hand and an incense burner in the other. Egzie Haraya prays with her hands held up in the Ethiopian way.

On the top of the roof of the church you can see a cross decorated with seven ostrich eggs.

Seven hundred years ago, there lived a man called Saga Zaab. He was rich, but he was holy too. His hymns were the sweetest, his prayers the humblest and his offerings the most generous in all Ethiopia.

Egzie Haraya, his wife, was an excellent housewife. Her pancakes were the finest, her woven cloth the softest, and her spicy stew the tastiest in all Ethiopia. Her husband loved her dearly, for she was beautiful and modest too.

Guests are sitting around the table at the feast. They are drinking honey mead out of the special flasks that Ethiopians still use today. They are eating round white pancakes with stew from the bowls in the middle of the table. In the picture below, you can see Egzie Haraya pouring out beer from a big clay pot. Saga Zaab will offer it to his guests.

But one thing made this perfect couple sad. Their fine, big house was quiet and empty. They did not have a child.

Every year Egzie Haraya gave food to the poor on the feast of St. Michael the Archangel, and prayed for a baby. But nothing happened.

So Saga Zaab gave half his goods to the church, and freed all his slaves, and prayed for a baby. But nothing happened.

Now there was in the country nearby a wicked king called Matalome. Strong and bold, cruel and ruthless, he rampaged about, and struck terror through the land.

One day, King Matalome and his horsemen came to Zorare, the town where Saga Zaab lived.

"The king is coming to kill you and steal all you have!" Saga Zaab's friends told him. "You must run away!"

So Saga Zaab ran as fast as he could. But he was not quite fast enough. Loud cries followed him. Hooves thundered behind him. Spears flew past his head. The horsemen came nearer and nearer. Saga Zaab came to the edge of a lake, and plunged straight in.

The water was cold and deep. Saga Zaab sank down into the depths. His lungs were bursting and he thought he would drown.

Then, just when he could swim no more, he came to a miraculous chamber of air under the water. And there before him was the Archangel Michael.

"Come in, Saga Zaab," said St. Michael.

So Saga Zaab went in, and he stayed for three days with the Archangel, and he told him all his troubles.

"Do not be sad," said the Archangel, "for you will have a son. He will be great, and holy, and a light to all the world."

Then the Archangel and the man swam up through the waters of the lake and the Archangel showed Saga Zaab the way to go home.

But when Saga Zaab came near to Zorare, his heart missed a beat, for he saw blackened ruins where houses and churches had been, and empty streets, where people and animals used to throng.

"My wife!" thought Saga Zaab. "Where is my wife?"

In Ethiopian pictures, the same person sometimes appears twice. Here you can see Saga Zaab swimming away from the horseman, and then safe in the arms of St. Michael. The horseman is wearing a warrior's leopard skin cloak and has armbands around his arms.

Egzie Haraya modestly covers her mouth with her veil. Her mule has the beautifully decorated bridle and richly patterned saddle cloth still used by important people in Ethiopia. The soldiers are carrying spears and shields.

He roamed through the ruins and called for her. "Wife! Dear wife! Where are you?"

But only crows and vultures squawked in reply.

Meanwhile, Egzie Haraya had been carried off by the captains of wicked King Matalome's horsemen. The captains saw how lovely she was, and their hearts were set on fire.

"Her hair is like the tendrils of twining plants," said one. "Let me take care of her."

"Her eyes sparkle with a bright, shining light," said another. "Let me carry her on my mule."

"Her neck is like a collar of gold," said a third. "Let me cover her with my cloak."

The king heard how beautiful and modest Egzie Haraya was.

"I'll marry her myself," he thought.

He did not care that Egzie Haraya was married already. He did not care that she sat all day, crying for her own dear husband. He sent her delicious food to eat. She refused to eat it. He sent her beautiful clothes to wear. She would not put them on.

"Enough of this!" cried the king. "She must do as she is told!"

His servants dressed the weeping lady in fine colored silks and covered her head with a gold embroidered veil.

"To the temple!" cried the king, "and let the wedding proceed!"

At the temple, a great crowd was gathered.

"The king! The king!" shouted everyone, and the women clacked their tongues in cries of welcome.

A thousand soldiers leaned on their spears ready to obey the king's commands, and three hundred magicians muttered their spells, holding up their magic charms.

A woman's wailing voice was heard above the noise, as Egzie Haraya was led protesting to the temple door.

"Here she comes! There she goes!" the wicked king's people said to each other. "It's a pity the veil falls over her face. We would have liked to see her cry."

Then suddenly, with a frightful crash, the air was split with noise. Thunder clapped and lightning struck. The earth quaked and the temple shook.

The people fell to the ground in terror, all except Egzie Haraya, for above her flew the Archangel Michael.

King Matalome, wearing a crown, falls back in fright at the sight of St. Michael. Wicked people in Ethiopian pictures are often painted from the side, with only one eye showing. Good people are always painted with their whole face showing.

Swooping down, he snatched her up and carried her off, and away she flew on his wings.

"What happened? What was that noise?" everyone said in fear and amazement.

But the one thousand soldiers said nothing at all. They had all been struck dead by lightning.

As for King Matalome, the shock had driven him mad. He returned to his palace and gave strange orders to his men.

"Kill all these people," he would say. "And build houses in the air."

"Yes, sire," his servants would answer politely. Then they went off and did nothing at all, and King Matalome never knew the difference.

The Archangel Michael set Egzie Haraya down at the door of the church where her husband was praying. She stood alone, and waited for him, her veil pulled over her face.

When Saga Zaab came out, he was surprised to see a lady standing there, all dressed in fine colored silks, with a gold embroidered veil pulled over her face.

"Who are you?" he said. He came a little nearer. "And why does such a lovely lady stand here all alone without a servant to look after her?"

Egzie Haraya was not very pleased.

"Perhaps he's forgotten me already," she thought, "and is looking for another wife."

So she kept her veil over her face and asked him clever questions. Saga Zaab answered all of them with sad sighs and shakes of the head.

"My own dear wife has disappeared," he said, "and I pray day and night that God will bring her back to me."

Egzie Haraya was overjoyed to hear this news. She flung back her veil, and ran into his arms, and they were the happiest couple in all Ethiopia.

On the left you can see the pillar of light that Egzie Haraya saw in her dream.
In the sky is the sun that Saga Zaab saw in his dream.

The next night, when they went to bed, Egzie Haraya fell asleep and dreamed of a pillar of light that stretched up to heaven from her own dear house, with birds in brilliant colors fluttering around it.

And as Saga Zaab slept he dreamed that the sun, trailing bright stars, rose from their bed and lit up the whole world.

Then the Archangel Michael appeared to the couple.

"You will have a son," he said, "beloved by God and honored by angels."

Nine months and five days later, Egzie Haraya had a beautiful baby boy. Saga Zaab was very happy. He made a great feast for the poor and needy. Egzie Haraya was happy too. She cuddled her baby and sang to him. She gave him her milk to drink, then she wrapped him in her shawl and tied him onto her back where he stayed all day, gurgling and smiling as she went about her work.

Egzie Haraya and Saga Zaab are in their house with their newborn son. Saga Zaab holds a strip of cloth in his hand. It shows that he is an important person. In Ethiopian pictures you will often see kings and other great men holding strips of cloth like this.

The child and his mother appear twice in this picture. First, the little boy fills the baskets with flour. Then his mother, her tears dried, runs to bring him the oil pots. A guardian angel watches from above.

The next year, trouble came again. There was a famine in the land. The grain jars were empty. The oil was all used up. Poor and rich alike had nothing left to eat.

Egzie Haraya was very sad. The day of the Archangel had come, and she had no food for the feast. She sat under a tree, and watched her baby play. He crawled into the house, and pointed to an empty basket.

"Are you hungry, little flower?" said his mother sadly.

The little boy put out a tiny hand to touch the basket, and then his mother gasped. What was this? Suddenly the basket was full! It was so heavy she could not hold it anymore! She lowered it to the ground and looked at the child in wonder. He had crawled away to the other baskets and as he touched each one, it overflowed with flour.

The child touches the oil pot. Later, Saga Zaab serves his guests from the big clay jar. It is polite in Ethiopia to take your cloak off your shoulders and wrap it round your waist when serving guests, as Saga Zaab has done.

"It's a miracle!" said Egzie Haraya in amazement. She ran to fetch her oil pot. Only a few drops were left in the bottom. The baby put one little hand inside, and his mother helped him to make the sign of the cross with the other. Then she gasped in wonder. Oil was bubbling up, filling the jar and frothing over.

Egzie Haraya's hands shook with excitement, and her heart sang with joy. She poured a little of the oil into each of her empty pots. In an instant, they were filled. Soon, she had all she needed for St. Michael's holy feast.

The famine was long and terrible, but while it lasted, the people of Zorare wanted for nothing. By the child's miraculous powers, they had food, and clothes, and everything they needed.

Saga Zaab sits in the covered chair of a great man while his son sits on the ground in front of him. Ethiopian children still learn the Bible in this way, resting their book or manuscript on a special wooden stand like this one. The pupil reads aloud from the book, and the teacher corrects him.

Now when the boy was seven, he began to learn his Bible.

"What a good memory he has!" his father said.

When he was fifteen, he became a deacon of the church.

"I see St. Michael beside him, holding a sword of fire," the bishop said.

When he was twenty-two, the Archangel Michael visited him, and Jesus appeared, seated upon the Archangel's wings.

"From now on, your name will be Tekla Haymanot," said the Archangel. "You will not hunt with a bow and spear like other young men, for you will be a priest. Go now, and perform miracles, and tell all the people of Ethiopia to mend their evil ways."

So Tekla Haymanot did as he was told, and everywhere he went, miracles took place, the sick were healed, and the dead rose again. And the people knew that he was a saint.

Both Jesus and St. Michael are holding up their hands in blessing. You will often see this sign in Ethiopian paintings.

The Saint (in the green robe) and Gebra Wahid (in the red loin cloth) are bound with ropes. The soldiers are wearing decorative armbands.

Now wicked King Matalome was still as mad and bad as ever. And when he heard that the Saint was going around telling people to mend their evil ways, he decided to kill him.

He sent for St. Tekla Haymanot and his good friend, Gebra Wahid, and putting them into wicker baskets, he tied the tops tightly and threw them off a high cliff. Three times he played the same trick, but each time St. Michael the Archangel swooped down and carried them to safety.

Then King Matalome tried to kill the Saint with his spear, but the spear bent in his hand. He had him tied up in prison, but the chains fell off his arms and legs.

Then the king called for his soldiers.

"What shall we do?" he asked them. "How shall we kill this magician?"

"Let's hang him from a tree," said the soldiers. "He won't escape us then."

"Very well," said the king. "But this time you must succeed."

The picture at the top shows the king asking for advice on how to kill St. Tekla Haymanot. In the picture on the left, the hangman appears twice, first up the tree, then lying dead at the bottom.

On the right, King Matalome's soldiers cut off the heads of all those who watched in wonder.

So King Matalome and his hangmen took the Saint, all bound in ropes, to a high tree, and there they hanged him. But the branch of the tree bent down low, and in the rustling of the leaves a voice was heard to say, "Descend from me, O man of God."

The tree set St. Tekla Haymanot gently on his feet, and the rope slipped off his neck, but the hangman tumbled off the highest branch and died.

Thousands of people watched in wonder, and fell down upon their knees, but this sent King Matalome into a violent rage, and he had all their heads cut off, for he was madder and more wicked than ever.

One day, Gebra Wahid, the friend of St. Tekla Haymanot, went to King Matalome, braving his violent anger.

"Why is it, O King," he said, "that you keep on fighting against this holy man? Why don't you ask him instead to heal your madness?"

"I would like to be healed," the king said slowly, "but I am afraid of Tekla Haymanot. Perhaps he will try to take away my kingdom."

At last Gebra Wahid persuaded King Matalome to call for the Saint. And St. Tekla Haymanot came, and offered up prayers to God, and immediately the king recovered from his madness.

In the olden days in Ethiopia, people were often baptized in rivers or lakes, in the same way that Jesus was baptized by St. John the Baptist.

And the Saint baptized the king with one hundred and two thousand and ninety-nine of his men, and the Saint taught the king about the Bible and showed him how to change his wicked ways. Then King Matalome was very sorry for all his evil deeds, and the innocent men he had put to death, and he decided to be good forevermore. The king and the Saint became friends, and talked for long hours about many things.

St. Tekla Haymanot travels from place to place on his carpet of light. He is wearing a bishop's headdress.

"Tell me," said the king one day. "Is it true that men can rise from the dead?"

"Yes," said St. Tekla Haymanot.

"Then show me," said the king. "One day, twenty-five years ago, a thousand of my soldiers were struck dead by lightning. Bring them back to life, and I will believe."

"Tell me first why they were killed," said Tekla Haymanot.

"I can't," said the king, and he looked down in shame.

"Then I'll tell you," said the Saint. "You stole a beautiful woman from her husband, and planned to marry her yourself. But St. Michael snatched her away from you, and struck your soldiers dead."

"How did you know?" the king said, thunderstruck.

"She was my mother," said St. Tekla Haymanot.

The king was horribly frightened when he heard this. He flung himself down at the Saint's bare feet, and his cheeks were streaked with tears of repentance.

"Forgive me," he said, "please, please forgive me."

"I forgive you," said the Saint, and he went to the place where the soldiers were buried, and their bones were knitted together again, and they all rose from the dead.

And Saint Tekla Haymanot went on his way, traveling on a carpet of light, which Jesus himself had given him. Everywhere he went, strange miracles happened, the sick were healed, and those who had died rose again.

A man brought his mule to the river to drink.

"Please wait until I have filled my water pot," said a woman. "Your mule will make the water dirty."

"No," said the man rudely.

"By St. Tekla Haymanot!" cried the woman, "Your mule shall not drink!" and although the man tried to force him, the mule refused to drink until the woman's pot was full.

A fierce leopard carried off a child.

"By our Father Tekla Haymanot, you shall not eat me!" cried out the little boy. The leopard carried him gently off to his den, and three days later the boy came home again, safe and sound, riding on the leopard's back.

A man was driving his cattle to drink in the river when a crocodile caught hold of an ox's leg.

"St. Tekla Haymanot, save him!" cried the man. The crocodile's teeth broke in his head, and the ox escaped unharmed.

St. Tekla Haymanot was climbing down the steep cliff below the great monastery of Debra Damo. Suddenly the rope broke. In an instant, six wings grew from his shoulders, and with them the Saint flew to safety.

Instead of celebrating the feast of St. Tekla Haymanot, a farmer went out to plough. At once a terrible hailstorm began. The huge hailstones stunned his oxen, and washed the earth away from his fields.

A vulture snatched a hen that a woman was preparing for the Saint's feast day.

"By St. Tekla Haymanot!" called the woman, "Bring me back my hen!" and the vulture brought it back. That hen had many chicks. One day some soldiers stole two of them and tried to cook them in a pot.

"By St. Tekla Haymanot! You shall not eat them!" cried the woman. The pot opened and the birds fluttered out alive.

Everywhere he went, St. Tekla Haymanot cast out devils, who rushed away from him. Many times, he brought the dead back to life.

Wild animals were eating up the crops.

"Let them eat," said the Saint. "They are God's creatures too." But a big ape attacked a poor widow and snatched away her food. So the Saint ordered all the wild animals to keep away from the fields, and they obeyed him.

Another time, a man with a horrible disease came to the cell of St. Tekla Haymanot. He washed in the stream nearby, and all his sores disappeared immediately.

Once, a giant two-horned snake tried to swallow St. Tekla Haymanot, but the Saint split the monster in two from head to tail. Satan, watching from far away, fled in terror.

A little boy climbed into a fire.

"St. Tekla Haymanot, save my child!" cried his mother in terror. The little boy was not hurt at all, but played with the flames, and not one hair of his head was singed. (If this miracle had not happened, the child would have been badly burned.)

A poor man suffered from a diseased hand. One day he was astonished to hear his mule and his donkey speak to him.

"Go to our Father Tekla Haymanot," they said, "and you will be cured."

The man did as they had told him, and his hand was healed.

The years passed, and the fame of the Saint spread far and wide. Many disciples came to him, and he taught them the ways of God. But as he grew old, the Saint grew tired.

"I have given light to the world," he said wearily, "but I have become darkness to myself. I have healed others, but I am sick myself."

So he left his followers, and went to a lonely place where he could devote himself to prayer. He made a tiny cell to live in, so small that he could neither sit down nor lie down. He even drove knives into the sides of it to force himself to stand. Year after year, day and night, St. Tekla Haymanot stood in his cell, eating and drinking almost nothing, praying to God without stopping.

After many years one of his legs withered and fell off, so the Saint stood on the other. For seven more years he stood there, asleep and awake, eating and drinking almost nothing, praying to God without ceasing.

The Saint is wearing the kind of garment with ropes across the chest that some monks and hermits still wear today.

The man painted across the bottom of the picture is probably the person who paid for this manuscript to be painted, and who wanted his own portrait to be included.

Then one day God sent his angels to take the Saint's soul to Heaven in a cloud of glory. And Jesus said to him, "You have kept faith, O good and faithful servant, and I will give you fifteen of the cities of Paradise, and five of the kingdoms of Heaven."

The soul of St. Tekla Haymanot, crowned and dressed in white, leaves his body, and is received by Jesus, who appears on a cloud of glory, bringing crowns for his faithful servant. On either side of the Saint stand the Archangels Gabriel and Michael.

St. Tekla Haymanot in Paradise with Jesus.

And when the Saint's soul had gone to Paradise, his grieving disciples buried his body in an open space, and a great monastery was built there. And it is still there to this very day, high up in the hills of Ethiopia, deep in the heart of Africa.